HOW DOES GOD GUIDE US?

Booklets taken from *Questions of Life:*

Is There More to Life Than This?

Who is Jesus?

Why Did Jesus Die?

How Can We Have Faith?

Why and How Do I Pray?

Why and How Should I Read the Bible?

How Does God Guide Us?

The Holy Spirit

How Can I Resist Evil?

Why and How Should I Tell Others?

Does God Heal Today?

What About the Church?

How Can I Make the Most of the Rest of My Life?

HOW DOES GOD GUIDE US?

NICKY GUMBEL

Alpha

ISBN: 978 1 907950 18 6

Published by Alpha International
Holy Trinity Brompton
Brompton Road
London SW7 1JA
Email: publications@alpha.org

Cover and text illustrations by Charlie Mackesy

CONTENTS

HOW DOES GOD GUIDE US?

We all have to make decisions in life. We are faced with decisions about relationships, marriage, children, use of time, jobs, homes, money, holidays, possessions, giving and so on. Some of these are big decisions; some are smaller. In many cases, it is of the utmost importance that we make the right decisions – for instance in our choice of a marriage partner. We need God's help.

One wonderful thing that the Christian faith shows us is that we are not on our own in this life. Guidance springs out of our relationship with God. He promises to guide those who are walking with him. He says: 'I will instruct you and teach you in the way you should go' (Psalm 32:8). Jesus promises to lead and guide his followers: 'He calls his own sheep by name and leads them out … His sheep follow him because they know his voice' (John 10:3–4). Jesus uses the analogy of a sheep with his shepherd to talk about the relationship that he wants to have with us. He longs for us to discover his will (Colossians 1:9; Ephesians 5:17). He is concerned for each of us as individuals. He loves us and wants to speak to us about what we should be doing with our lives – about little things as well as big things.

God has a plan for our lives (Ephesians 2:10). Sometimes people are worried by this. They think, 'I'm not sure that I want God's plan for my life. Will his plans be good?' We need not fear. God loves us and wants the very best for our lives. Paul tells us that God's will for our lives is 'good, pleasing and perfect' (Romans 12:2). He said to his people through the prophet Jeremiah: '"For I know the plans I have for you," declares the Lord, "plans to prosper you and not to harm you, plans to give you hope and a future"' (Jeremiah 29:11). He is saying, 'Don't you realise that I have a really good plan for your life? I have prepared something wonderful.' This cry from God's heart came because he saw the mess his people had got themselves into when they didn't follow his plans. All around us we see people whose lives are in a muddle. After they have come to Christ people often say to me, 'I wish I had become a Christian five or ten years earlier. Look at my life now. It is such a mess.'

If we are to find out about God's plans for us, we need to ask him about them. God warned his people about embarking on plans without consulting him: '"Woe to the obstinate children," declares the Lord, "to those who carry out plans that are not mine … who go down to Egypt *without consulting me*"'(Isaiah 30:1–2, italics mine). Of course, Jesus is the supreme example of doing the will of his Father. He was consistently 'led by the Spirit'(Luke 4:1) and only did what he saw his Father doing (John 5:19).

Sometimes we make mistakes because we fail to consult God. We make a plan and think, 'I want to do that but I am not quite sure whether God wants me to do it. I think I'd better not ask him, just in case it's not his will for me!'

God guides us when we are prepared to do his will rather than insisting that our own way is right. The psalmist says, 'He guides the humble' (Psalm 25:9) and 'confides in those who fear [respect] him' (v.14). God guides those whose attitude is like Mary's: 'I am the Lord's servant and I am willing to do whatever he wants' (Luke 1:38, TLB). The moment we are prepared to do his will, he begins to reveal his plans for our lives.

There is a verse in the Psalms, which I go back to time and time again: 'Commit your way to the Lord; trust in him, and he will act' (Psalm 37:5, RSV). Our part is to commit the decision to the Lord and then to trust him. When we have done that, we can wait expectantly for him to act.

Towards the end of our time at university, a friend of mine called Nicky, who had become a Christian about the same time that I did, became very close to a girl who was not a Christian. He felt it was not right to marry her unless she shared his faith in Christ. He did not want to put her under any pressure. So he did what the psalmist said and committed it to the Lord. He said, in effect, 'Lord, if this relationship is not right, I pray that you will stop it. If it is right, then I pray she will become a Christian by the last day of the Spring term.' He did not tell her, or anyone else, about this date. He put his 'trust in him' and waited for God to act. The final day of the Spring term arrived and they

happened to be going to a party together that night.
Just before midnight, she told him she wanted to go
for a drive. So they got into the car and she gave him a
whole string of directions off the top of her head, just
for fun: 'Three turnings left, three turnings right, drive
straight for three miles and stop.' He played along
and followed them. They ended up in the American
cemetery which has one enormous cross in the centre,
surrounded by hundreds of little crosses. She was
shocked and deeply moved by the symbol of the cross,
and also by the fact that God had used her instructions
to get her attention. She burst into tears. Moments
later, she came to faith in Christ. They have now been
happily married for many years and still look back
and remember how God's hand was on them at that
moment.

Given that we are willing to do what God wants us
to do, in what ways should we expect God to speak to
us and guide us? There are various ways in which he
guides us. Sometimes God speaks through one of the
ways set out below; sometimes it is a combination. If it
is a major decision, he may speak through all of them.
They are sometimes called the five 'CSs'.

Commanding scripture

As we have seen, God's general will for all people
in all places and all circumstances is revealed in
Scripture. In the Bible God has told us what he thinks
about a whole range of issues. We know from the
Bible that certain things are wrong. We can therefore
be quite sure that God will not guide us to do these

things. Sometimes a married person says, 'I have fallen in love with this man/woman. We love each other so much. I feel God is leading me to leave my husband/wife and to start this new relationship.' But God has already made his will clear. He has said, 'You shall not commit adultery' (Exodus 20:14).

Sometimes people feel led to save money by not paying their income tax. But God has made it clear that we are to pay any taxes that are due (Romans 13:7). I came across a letter that was written to the Inland Revenue by a man who had just become a Christian. He wrote: 'Dear Sir, I have just become a Christian and have found that I cannot sleep at night. So here is a hundred pounds that I owe you. PS If I still can't sleep, I'll send you the rest.'

God also calls us to be people of integrity and tell the truth (Exodus 20:16). I remember once meeting an old man whose nickname was Gibbo. Many years before, he had worked as a clerk in Selfridges, the famous London department store. His boss was the founder, Gordon Selfridge. One day the phone rang; Gibbo picked it up and the caller asked to speak to Gordon Selfridge. Selfridge was in the room, but when Gibbo motioned to him, he said, 'Tell him I'm out.' Gibbo handed him the phone and said, 'You tell him you're out!' After he put the phone down, Selfridge was furious. But Gibbo stood his ground and said to him, 'If I can lie for you, I can lie to you and I never will.' This action transformed Gibbo's career at Selfridges. From that moment on, when his employers needed someone they could really trust, they turned to him. He had proved his integrity.

In these, and many other areas, God has revealed his general will. We do not need to ask for his guidance because he has already given it. If we are not sure, we may need to ask someone who knows the Bible better than we do whether there is anything addressing that issue. Once we have discovered what the Bible says, we need search no further.

Although God's general will is revealed in the Bible, we cannot always find his particular will for our lives there. It does not tell us which job we should do, how much money we should give away, or whom we should marry.

We discussed in the booklet *Why and How Should I Read the Bible?*, how God still speaks through the Scriptures today. He may speak to us as we read. The psalmist says, 'Your statutes … are my counsellors' (Psalm 119:24). That is not to say that we find God's will by opening the Bible at random and seeing what it says. Rather, if we get into a regular Bible reading habit, sometimes it can be quite extraordinary how appropriate each day's reading seems to be for our own particular circumstances.

Sometimes a verse seems almost to leap out of the page at us and we sense God speaking through it. This was certainly my experience when I sensed God calling me to change jobs. The choice I faced was between carrying on with law, or becoming a vicar. Each time I felt God speaking to me as I read the Bible, I wrote it down. On one occasion, for example, when I had been praying to God to guide me, I read the verse, 'How can they believe in the one of whom they have not heard? And how can they hear without someone

12

preaching to them?' (Romans 10:14). This happened on a Thursday. I then drove to Durham for the weekend to see some friends and pray about the decision I had to make. Out of the blue, my friend read out that verse. I was amazed! On the Sunday evening, I was at church back in London. At the beginning of the service my vicar at the time announced not only that he was to be preaching on this same verse but, that through it he felt God was calling somebody to ordination in the Church of England. I noted at least fifteen different occasions in which I believe God spoke to me through the Bible about this call.

Compelling Spirit

Guidance is very personal. When we become Christians, the Spirit of God comes to live within us. When he does so, he begins to communicate with us. We need to learn to hear his voice. Jesus said that his sheep (his followers) would recognise his voice (John 10:4–5). We recognise a good friend's voice immediately on the phone. If we do not know the person so well, it may be harder and take more time. The more we get to know Jesus, the easier we will find it to recognise his voice.

St Paul says, 'And now, compelled by the Spirit, I'm going to Jerusalem.' Paul's expectation was that all Christians were led by the Spirit (Galatians 5:18). On another occasion, we find Paul and his companions planning to enter Bithynia, 'but the Spirit of Jesus would not allow them to' (Acts 16:7). So they went a different way. We do not know exactly how the

Spirit spoke to them, but it may have been in one of a number of ways.

Here are three examples of ways in which God speaks by his Spirit.

1. God often speaks to us as we pray

In Acts 13, we read that 'as they were worshipping the Lord, the Holy Spirit spoke to them.' Prayer is a two-way conversation. Suppose I go to the doctor and say, 'Doctor, I have a number of problems: I have fungus growing under my toenails, my eyes itch, I need a flu jab, I have very bad backaches and I have tennis elbow.' Then, having got through my list of complaints, I look at my watch and say, 'Goodness me, time is getting on. Well, I must be off. Thanks very much for listening.' The doctor might want to say, 'Hang on a second. Do you not want to hear what I have to say?' If, whenever we pray, we only speak to God and never take time to listen, we make the same mistake. It's for this reason that I have a notebook next to me when I pray. I find it helpful to jot down thoughts that come into my mind like, 'perhaps I should ring or write to that person'.

In the Bible we find God speaking to his people. For example, on one occasion as the Christians were worshipping the Lord and fasting, the Holy Spirit said, '"Set apart for me Barnabas and Saul for the work to which I have called them." So after they had fasted and prayed, they placed their hands on them and sent them off' (Acts 13:2–3).

Again, we don't know exactly how the Holy Spirit spoke. It may be that as they were praying the thought

14

came into their minds. That is a common way in which God speaks. People sometimes describe it as 'impressions' or 'knowing it deep down'. It is possible for the Holy Spirit to speak in all of these ways.

Obviously such thoughts and feelings need to be tested (1 John 4:1). Is the impression in line with the Bible? Does it promote love? If it does not, it cannot come from a God who is love (1 John 4:16). Is it strengthening, encouraging and comforting (1 Corinthians 14:3)? When we have made the decision, do we know God's peace (Colossians 3:15)?

2. God sometimes speaks to us by giving us a strong desire to do something

'God … works in you to *will* and to act according to his good purpose' (Philippians 2:13, italics mine). As we surrender our wills to God, he works in us and often changes our desires.

A young British doctor called Paul Brand was once visiting a leprosy sanatorium near Chennai (formerly Madras), India. As he was being shown around the hospital by a man called Dr Cochrane, he saw patients who were squatting and stumping along on bandaged feet, following the two doctors with their unseeing, deformed faces. Dr Paul Brand said this:

> Hands waved at me and stretched out in greeting … They were twisted, gnarled, ulcerated stumps. Some were stiff like metal claws. Some were missing fingers. Some hands were missing altogether. Finally I could restrain myself no longer. 'How did they get this way? What do you do about them?' … [Dr

Cochrane said,] 'I don't know … I am a skin man – I can treat that part of the leprosy. But you are a bone man, the orthopaedic surgeon!'… He went on to tell me that not one orthopaedic surgeon had yet studied the deformities of the fifteen million leprosy victims in the world.

As they were passing, a young person who had leprosy put out his hand, and Paul Brand said to him, 'Squeeze my hand as hard as you can.' He has said of that encounter:

To my amazement instead of the twitch I'd expected to feel, this sharp and intense pain raced through my palm. His grip was like a vice, with fingers digging into my flesh like steel talons. He showed no paralysis – in fact, I cried out for him to let go. I looked up angrily, but was alarmed by the gentle smile on his face. He didn't know he was hurting me. That was the clue: somewhere in that severely deformed hand were powerfully good muscles. I felt a tingling, as if the whole universe was revolving around me. I knew I had arrived in my place. That single incident in 1947 changed my life. It was my moment. I'd felt a call of the Spirit of God. I was made for that one moment, and knew that I would have to point my life in a new direction. I've never doubted it since.[1]

Dr Brand went on to discover that leprosy destroyed the sensation of pain in affected parts of the body, so patients inadvertently injured and destroyed themselves. This was entirely due to infection, and thus preventable. This led to pioneering research into the disease, and Dr Brand became a world-renowned leprosy surgeon, receiving a CBE and the Albert Lasker award.

3. God sometimes guides in more unusual ways

There are many examples in the Bible of God guiding individuals in dramatic ways. When Samuel was a small boy, God spoke to him in such a way that he was able to physically hear God's words with his own ears (1 Samuel 3:4–14). He guided Abraham (Genesis 18), Joseph (Matthew 2:19) and Peter (Acts 12:7) through angels. In both the Old Testament and the New Testament (eg, Agabus – Acts 11:27–28; 21:10–11) God often spoke through prophets. He guided through visions (sometimes referred to today as 'pictures'). For example, one night God spoke to Paul in a vision. He saw a man in Macedonia standing and begging him, 'Come over to Macedonia and help us.' Not surprisingly, Paul and his companions took this as guidance that God had called them to preach the gospel in Macedonia (Acts 16:10).

We also find examples of God guiding through dreams (eg, Matthew 1:20; 2:12–13, 22). I was praying for a couple who were good friends of ours. The husband had recently come to faith in Christ. The wife was highly intelligent, but strongly against what had happened to her husband. She became a little hostile towards us. One night I had a dream in which I saw her face quite changed, her eyes full of the joy of the Lord. This encouraged us to continue praying and keeping close to both of them. A few months later she came to faith in Christ. I remember looking at her and seeing the face I had seen in the dream a few months earlier.

These are all ways in which God has guided people in the past, and how he still does today.

Common sense

When we become Christians, we are not called to abandon common sense. The New Testament writers often encourage us to think and never discourage us from using our minds (eg, 2 Timothy 2:7).

If we abandon common sense, then we get ourselves into absurd situations. In his book *Knowing God*, J. I. Packer quotes an example of a woman who each morning, having consecrated the day to the Lord as soon as she woke, 'would then ask him whether she was to get up or not', and would not stir till 'the voice' told her to dress.

> As she put on each article she asked the Lord whether she was to put it on and very often the Lord would tell her to put on the right shoe and leave off the other; sometimes she was to put on both stockings and no shoes; and sometimes both shoes and no stockings. It was the same with all the articles of dress ... [2]

It is true to say that God's promises of guidance were not given so that we could avoid the strain of thinking. Indeed, John Wesley, the father of Methodism, said that God usually guided him by presenting reasons to his mind for acting in a certain way. This is important in every area, both in the ordinary day-to-day decisions of life, but also concerning marriage and jobs. Common sense is one of the factors to be taken into account in the whole area of choosing a marriage partner for life. It is common sense to look at least three important aspects.

First, are we *spiritually compatible*? Paul warns of the danger of marrying someone who is not a Christian (2 Corinthians 6:14). In practice, if one of the parties is not a Christian, it nearly always leads to a great tension in the marriage. This happens because the two people are going in different directions. The Christian feels torn between the desire to serve their spouse and their desire to serve the Lord. However, spiritual compatibility means more than the fact that both are Christians. It means that each party respects the other's faith, rather than simply being able to say, 'At least they pass the test of being a Christian.'

Second, are we *personally compatible*? Obviously, our spouse should be a very good friend and someone with whom we have a great deal in common. One of the many advantages of not sleeping together before getting married is that it is easier to concentrate on the area of personal compatibility. Often the sexual side can dominate the early stages of a relationship. If the foundations have not been built on friendship then, when the initial sexual excitement wears off, it can leave the relationship without a solid base.

Third, are we *physically compatible*? By this I mean that we should be attracted to each other. It is not enough to be spiritually and emotionally compatible.

19

Often people put sexual compatibility first, but this comes last in the order of priorities. Is it necessary to sleep together in order to see whether there is sexual compatibility? No, this approach begs the question, how many sexual encounters do we need before we can make a rationally informed choice?

Again, common sense is vital when considering God's guidance about our jobs and careers. Sometimes people say, 'I've become a Christian. Should I leave my job?' The answer is given by Paul: '… retain the place in life that the Lord has assigned to you and to which God has called you' (1 Corinthians 7:17). Unless our job is totally incompatible with the Christian faith, St Paul is telling us to live out the Christian life in whatever setting that call took place.

The general rule is that we should stay in our current job (if we are in employment) until God calls us to do something else. God does not tend to call us *out of* things, rather he calls us *into* things. To discern what God might be calling us into, we should ask ourselves, 'What is my temperament? What is my personality? What am I good at? What do I like doing? What are my gifts?' It is also common sense to take a long-term view of life. It is wise to look ahead ten, fifteen, twenty years and ask the questions: 'Where is my present job taking me? Is that where I want to go in the long term? Or is my long-term vision for something quite different? In which case, where should I be now in order to get there?'

Counsel of the saints

The word 'saints' is used in the New Testament to mean 'all Christians' – in other words, the church (eg, Philippians 1:1). It is wonderful to be part of a community of Christians, in which we can help one another in making our decisions. We need to have the humility to recognise that God does not just speak to 'me', but that he also speaks to other people, and he has done so through history.

The Book of Proverbs is full of injunctions to seek wise advice. The writer asserts that 'the wise listen to advice' (Proverbs 12:15). He warns that 'plans fail for lack of counsel', but on the other hand, 'with many advisers they succeed' (Proverbs 15:22). Therefore, he urges, 'make plans by seeking advice' (Proverbs 20:18).

While seeking advice is very important, we need

to remember that, ultimately, our decisions are between us and God. They are our responsibility. We cannot shift that responsibility onto others or seek to blame them if things go wrong. The 'counsel of the saints' is part of guidance – but it is not the only part. Sometimes it may be right to go ahead in spite of the advice of others.

If we are faced with a decision and we need advice, whom should we consult? To the writer of Proverbs, 'The fear of the Lord is the beginning of wisdom …' (Proverbs 9:10). Probably, therefore, he is thinking of advice from those who fear or respect the Lord. The best advisers are often people whom we respect; they are usually godly Christian people with wisdom and experience. It may also be wise to seek the advice of our parents, even if we no longer live at home. They probably know us better than anyone else, and in asking them we honour them (Exodus 20:12).

I have found it a real help throughout my Christian life to have someone to whom I can go for advice on a whole range of issues: a mature Christian whom I respect. At different times I have turned to different people. I am so grateful to God for their wisdom and help in many areas. Often God's insight came as we talked through the issues together.

When it comes to bigger decisions, I have found it helpful to seek a range of advice. Over the question of ordination, I sought the advice of two such men, my two closest friends, my vicar and those who were involved in the official process of selection.

The people whom we ask for advice should not be chosen on the basis that they will agree with what

we have already planned to do! Sometimes one sees
a person consulting countless people in the hope that
they will eventually find somebody who will endorse
their plans. Such advice has little weight and simply
enables the person to say, 'I consulted x and he or
she agreed.' We should consult people on the basis
of their spiritual authority, or their relationship to us,
regardless of what we may anticipate their views to
be.

Circumstantial signs

God is in ultimate control of all events. The writer of
Proverbs points out: 'In your heart you may plan your
course, but the Lord determines your steps' (Proverbs
16:9). Sometimes God opens doors (1 Corinthians 16:9)
and sometimes he closes them (Acts 16:7). There have
been two occasions in my life when God has closed
the door on something which I very much wanted,
and which I believed at the time was God's will. I tried
to force the doors open. I prayed and I struggled and
I fought, but they would not open. On both occasions
I was bitterly disappointed. But I understand now,
years later, why he closed those doors. Indeed I am
grateful that he did. However, I am not sure I will ever
know, this side of heaven, why God has closed certain
doors in my life.

Sometimes he opens doors in a remarkable way.
The circumstances and the timing point clearly to the
hand of God (eg, Genesis 24). Michael Bourdeaux is
head of Keston College, a research unit devoted to
helping Christians in what were communist lands. His

work and research are respected by governments all over the world. He studied Russian at Oxford and his Russian teacher, Dr Zernov, sent him a letter which he had received because he thought it would interest him. It detailed how monks were being beaten up by the KGB and subjected to inhuman medical examinations; how they were being rounded up in lorries and dumped many hundreds of miles away. The letter was written very simply, with no adornment, and as he read it Michael Bourdeaux felt he was hearing the true voice of the persecuted church. The letter was signed 'Varavva and Pronina'.

In August 1964, he went on a trip to Moscow, and on his first evening there met up with old friends who explained that the persecutions were getting worse; in particular the old church of St Peter and St Paul had been demolished. They suggested that he go to see it for himself.

So he took a taxi, arriving at dusk. When he came to the square where he had remembered a very beautiful church, he found nothing except a twelve-foot-high fence which hid the rubble where the church had been. Over on the other side of the square, climbing the fence to try to see what was inside, were two women. He watched them, and when they finally left the square he followed them for a hundred yards and eventually caught up with them. They asked, 'Who are you?' He replied, 'I am a foreigner. I have come to find out what is happening here in the Soviet Union.'

They took him back to the house of another woman who asked him why he had come. He said he had received a letter from the Ukraine via Paris. When she asked who it was from, he replied, 'Varavva and Pronina.' There was silence. He wondered if he had said something wrong. There followed a flood of uncontrolled sobbing. The woman pointed and said, 'This is Varavva, and this is Pronina.'

The population of Russia is over 140 million. The Ukraine, from where the letter was written, is 1,300 kilometres from Moscow. Michael Bourdeaux had flown from England six months after the letter had been written. They would not have met had either party arrived at the demolished church an hour earlier or an hour later. That was one of the ways God called Michael Bourdeaux to set up his life's work, Keston College.[3]

Sometimes God's guidance seems to come as soon as it is asked for (eg, Genesis 24), but often it takes much longer; sometimes months or even years. We may have a sense that God is going to do something in our lives, but have to wait a long time for it to happen. On these occasions we need patience like that of Abraham who 'after waiting patiently… received what was promised'(Hebrews 6:15). He spent most of his life waiting for God to fulfil a promise he had given him when he was a young man, which was not fulfilled until he was an old man. While waiting, he was tempted at one point to try and force the issue, to fulfil God's promises by his own means – with disastrous results (see Genesis 16 and 21).

Sometimes we hear God correctly, but we get the timing wrong. God spoke to Joseph in a dream about what would happen to him and his family. He probably expected immediate fulfilment, but he had to wait years. Indeed, while he was in prison it must have been hard for him to believe that his dreams would ever be fulfilled. But thirteen years after the original dream, he saw God's fulfilment. The waiting was part of the preparation (see Genesis 37–50).

In this area of guidance, we all make mistakes. Sometimes, like Abraham, we try to fulfil God's purpose by our own wrong methods. Like Joseph, we get the timing wrong. Sometimes we feel that we have made too much of a mess of our lives by the time we come to Christ for God to do anything with us. But God is greater than that. Oscar Wilde, author and playwright, said, 'Every saint has a past, and every sinner has a future.'[4] God is able to 'restore to you the years which the swarming locust has eaten' (Joel 2:25, RSV). He is able to make something good out of whatever is left of our lives – whether it is a short time or a long time – if we will offer what we have to him and co operate with his Spirit.

Lord Radstock was staying in a hotel in Norway in the mid-nineteenth century. He heard a little girl playing the piano down in the hallway. She was making a terrible noise: 'Plink … plonk … plink … ' It was driving him mad! A man came and sat beside her and began playing alongside her, filling in the gaps. The result was the most beautiful music. He later discovered that the man playing alongside was the girl's father, Alexander Borodin, composer of the opera *Prince Igor*.

Paul writes that 'in all things God works for the good of those who love him, who have been called according to his purpose' (Romans 8:28). As we falteringly play our part – seeking his will for our lives by reading (commanding Scripture), listening (compelling Spirit), thinking (common sense), talking (counsel of the saints), watching (circumstantial signs) and waiting – God comes and sits alongside us 'and in all things … works for the good'. He takes our 'plink … plonk … plonk … 'and makes something beautiful out of our lives.

NOTES

1. Philip Yancey and Paul Brand, *In the Likeness of God* (Zondervan, 2004) p.218.
2. J. I. Packer, *Knowing God* (Hodder & Stoughton, 1973).
3. Michael Bourdeaux, *Risen Indeed* (Darton, Longman & Todd, 1983).
4. Oscar Wilde, *The Importance of Being Earnest and Other Plays*, ed. Richard Allen Cave (London, Penguin Classics, 2000) p.147.

THE ALPHA COURSE

The Alpha course is a practical introduction to the Christian faith, initiated by Holy Trinity Brompton in London and now being run by thousands of churches, of many denominations, throughout the world. If you are interested in finding out more about the Christian faith and would like details of your nearest Alpha course, please visit our website

alpha.org
or contact:

The Alpha Office,
Holy Trinity Bompton,
Brompton Road, London,
SW7 1JA
Tel: 0845 644 7544
Email: info@alpha.org

ALPHA TITLES AVAILABLE

Why Jesus?   A booklet – given to all participants at the start of the Alpha course. 'The clearest, best illustrated and most challenging short presentation of Jesus that I know.' – Michael Green

Why Christmas?   The Christmas version of *Why Jesus?*

Questions of Life   The Alpha course in book form. In fifteen compelling chapters Nicky Gumbel points the way to an authentic Christianity which is exciting and relevant to today's world.

Searching Issues   The seven issues most often raised by participants on the Alpha course: suffering, other religions, sex before marriage, the New Age, homosexuality, science and Christianity, and the Trinity.

A Life Worth Living   What happens after Alpha? Based on the book of Philippians, this is an invaluable next step for those who have just completed the Alpha course, and for anyone eager to put their faith on a firm biblical footing.

The Jesus Lifestyle   Studies in the Sermon on the Mount showing how Jesus' teaching flies in the face of a modern lifestyle and presents us with a radical alternative.

The Heart of Revival   Ten Bible studies based on the book of Isaiah, drawing out important truths for today by interpreting some of the teaching of the Old Testament prophet Isaiah. The book seeks to understand what revival might mean and how we can prepare to be part of it.

30 Days   Nicky Gumbel selects thirty passages from the Old and New Testament which can be read over thirty days. It is designed for those on an Alpha course and others who are interested in beginning to explore the Bible.

All titles are by Nicky Gumbel, who is Vicar of Holy Trinity Brompton